SOCIOLOGY
OF RELIGION

Georg Simmel

SOCIOLOGY
OF RELIGION

Translated from the German

by

CURT ROSENTHAL

———

PHILOSOPHICAL LIBRARY
New York

Type set at the Polyglot Press, New York
Printed in the United States of America

Translator's Note

The difficulties and exasperations accruing in the translation of a German scholar are vividly described by the translators of the writings of Max Weber. In discussing the style of German professors they comment: "They use parentheses, qualifying clauses, inversions and complex rhythmic devices in their polyphonic sentences. . . . At their best, they erect a grammatical edifice, in which mental balconies and watchtowers, as well as bridges and recesses, decorate the main structure."

This poetic and euphemistic characterization holds true also for the style of Georg Simmel. Sentences of breathtaking length are followed by phrases of even longer periods. Worse, ever repeated relative pronouns refer to subjects many sentences back, and the reader, caught in the entanglement of grammatical structure, is often forced to retrace the whole paragraph, to rediscover the lost trend of thought.

In my translation I have tried to disentangle these distracting agglomerations. I have co-ordinated subordinate phrases, long sentences have been broken up. Whenever feasible, I have repeated the noun, whereas Simmel prefers the relative pronoun. I have tried to find unequivocal expressions where Simmel resorts to ambiguous words.

And yet it remains rough going. But I hope the reader will be rewarded for whatever shortcomings the style may still have, by the author's abundance of ideas and insights.

C. R.

INTRODUCTION

Georg Simmel belongs to a generation which gave us great sociologists. He himself was a leading one who, specifically, represents the continental, particularly German tradition. His approach and theoretical treatment are close to philosophy, with a flair for wide synthesis.

Simmel's systematic sociology is based on his formal analysis of social relations, such as domination, coordination, subordination, and superordination of individuals and groups, always conscious of the size of the group involved. His well-known study of dyads and triads in which he saw significant differences in the relationships of the individuals involved, is of this order. As a matter of fact, it was these studies which paved the way for our concepts of small group development.

In addition to his formalism, his studies of synthesis on a wide scale, to which his sociology of religion belongs, may be found again in the outstanding writings of L. von Wiese. Simmel was a man of unusual talents, lecturing, researching and writing in many fields. Kurt Wolff who translated his writings into English, mentions as fields to which he devoted himself, among others, logic, the principles of philosophy, modern philosophy, the philosophy of religion and of art, ethics, social psychology, political psychology, and sociology.

His philosophical training and interest are always apparent in his writings. His sociology borders on philosophy. He tends toward generalizations and abstractions often far removed from the concrete and factual. But it is, perhaps, due to his philosophic bent that his writings abound in new ideas and concepts and theories.

The *Sociology of Religion* definitely belongs amongst his works which reflect his philosophical, even theological interest. Sometimes we may be in doubt as to how to classify his writings. For Simmel, religion is a reality related to the empirical. It is reflected in social relationships, while certain other social relationships not ordinarily recognized as such, are of a religious character. Much like Durkheim, Simmel discovers in religion an integrating, unifying element. Religion welds human society together and comes to the fore in social behavior, in customs and social interplay. Having taken up the discussion of the significance of the concept of faith, Simmel characteristically moves on to some of the basic social processes discoverable in competition and the division of labor. Competition he takes as a dividing force in that it alienates individuals, while division of labor has the tendency to unify. Religious avocations, such as becoming a priest, as well as certain other functions connected with religion, are the results of the unifying tendency inherent in the social division of labor. Religious ideas and their systematization, argues Simmel, do not contain divisive elements. Their basic characteristics tend in the direction of unity. Religion, in Simmel's theory, is, in fact, the highest expression of the concept of social unity. This may be seen especially in the old Roman religion with its drive toward family unity, and in Christianity with its universalistic ideas sponsoring the unity of all mankind.

Simmel's analysis of religion is, fundamentally, an analysis of the Judeo Christian religious complex, with a few digressions into other religions. Thus, the dominant values which Simmel recognizes in religion, may be identified with the Judeo-Christian religion.

Some of the findings of Simmel's are similar to those of Weber and Durkheim. His main thesis that religion is reflected in social relationships, is, basically, not so different from Max Weber's approach in his study of the sociology of religions. The integrative quality of religion was also stressed by Durkheim. But the style and the development of ideas are different in Simmel.

First of all, Simmel develops his ideas far more abstractly and not in contact with the empirical as did Weber and Durkheim. Moreover, Simmel does not make any attempt at a purely empirical and functional explanation of religion, nor does he try to discover the origins and causes of religion. Rather, his search is in line with theological, transcendental reasoning which is incapable of evaluation by empirical standards.

This book is not easy reading. Let us remember that Simmel wrote at a time and in an environment where the mode of thinking and the style of expressing one's ideas exhibited a certain disregard for clarity which was not only characteristic but highly respectable among academicians and intellectuals. He also lived at a time of turmoil.

Simmel was born in 1858. His studies were mainly history and philosophy. Inspite of his brilliant lectures at the university and his important contributions in the fields mentioned above, he remained for most of his life a Privat-Dozent. Very late in life he was awarded an honorary professorial title at the University of Berlin, and just four years prior to his death he was appointed a full professor at the University of Strassburg. At the beginning of World War I, Simmel was carried away by German nationalism, unlike some others, W. E. Forster among them, to whom nationalistic slogans made no appeal whatever. Simmel died of cancer in 1918 after meticulously arranging all his affairs.

Brooklyn College   Feliks Gross

Powers of a personal or objective order, interfering to any degree in our lives, are sometimes felt as inconvenient or improper. They immediately lose this character of interference, however, once the rate of their stress or their claims are increased. Its partial and relatively uncongenial value for the other elements of life, with which it is intertwined, may gain an absolute and dominant importance and for them an organic, satisfactory relation. Often a love, an ambition, a newly emerging interest will not co-ordinate the already existing purposes of life; but as soon as passion or determination integrates them into the center of the soul, and harmonizes the totality of our existence with them, there arises on this totally new basis an altogether novel life of a potentially homogeneous character.

Theoretical relations in regard to objects assimilate this phenomenon of the practical. The problem of the interaction of corporeal and spiritual existence troubled the thoughts of the philosophers. Spinoza solved that incompatibility by proving that extension on the one side and consciousness on the other—each in its own language—express the totality of existence; they become compatible as soon as they no longer intermingle as relative elements, but each claims

1

for itself the totality of the universe, and depicts it, in its own manner, as a whole. Maybe this development can also unravel certain of the theoretical difficulties of religion, as it has already aided in the solution of conflicts within the religious life. The ideals and aspirations of religion clash not only with impulses of a low order, but often also with norms and values of a spiritual and moral order.

A way out of such derangements and confusions was found by giving the former claims a relatively larger role, thus establishing them as absolute. Only when religion is the deciding factor in life, can it relate life's separate elements truly to each other or to the whole. And if the concept of the religious is formed accordingly, it may clear up the contradictions in which the categories of the balance of life usually involve this antagonism. That does not, however, imply an autocracy of religious thought by the suppression of other spheres of interest; for each of the great forms of our existence has to be proved capable of expressing the totality of life in its own language. The organization of our existence through the absolute domination by one principle of all the others would thus be elevated to a higher level: each of them—by its sovereignly formed world-picture— would be freed of the fear of any intrusion by the others; for each grants to these other elements the same right to fashion their own world. In principle they are as incommensurable as sounds and colors. This congruence is vouched for on the one hand by the unity of content which manifests itself in all these differentiated forms, and on the other by the unilateral course of the spiritual life. For, from the multiplicity of those worlds, which lie, as it were, before and in us as ideal potentialities, it takes only fragments to form its unity—although the pursuit of its changing goals may cause clashes of severe conflict.

For a naïve man the world of experience and practice is reality *as such*. The phenomena of the world exist as perceivable and manageable facts. Insofar as they are perceived as categories of art or religion, of values of awareness or philosophical speculation, they are made to confront that exclusively operating existence by which they realign themselves with the multiplicity of life—just as the course of individual existence is intermingled with the fragments of foreign or even hostile elements, to produce a whole. Thus arise the uncertainties and confusions in concepts of the world and life, immediately cleared up by the ready acceptance of so-called "reality" as a form under which we systematize given contents—contents which we can arrange artistically or religiously, scientifically or playfully.

"Reality" is not at all *the* world as such, but only one world, augmented by the world of art as well as religion, made up of the same material, but according to different forms and different presuppositions. The empirical real world means probably that order of given elements which is for practical purposes conditioned to the maintenance and development of the life of the species. In our behavior we experience reactions to the surrounding world; the usefulness or harm of these reactions depend on our notions, which induce us to action in turn. We call reality only that world, or that manner of conception, which we find at the

3

root of our actions in accordance with the particularity which furthers and preserves our specific characteristics and psychobiological organization. For differently organized beings with different needs there exists a different "reality," because their condition of life requires different actions, i.e., actions based on different considerations.

Thus the ends and the principal presuppositions are decisive for the kind of "world" our soul frames for itself. The "real" world, however, is only one of many possible ones. By its very nature our life needs for its practical support additional aliments, which are instrumental in creating other worlds. Art too lives by the elementary aspects of reality; but it becomes art by shaping them according to the artistic needs of viewing, of feeling, of significance, which lie entirely beyond those of reality. Is not the space depicted in a picture of a quite different shape than the space of reality? Visible unity and its mental expression in art vary indeed from the forms of reality—otherwise there would be no need for art to complement reality. One might call art a specific logic, a specific concept of the truth, a specific method, of placing next to the world of reality a new universe constructed of the same materials and equal to it.

The same probably holds true also of religion. Out of the visible and the conceptual, which we also experience in the realm of reality, the religious world arises in new tensions, new extensions and new syntheses. The concepts of soul and existence, of destiny and guilt, of happiness and sacrifice, even of the hair on our head and of the sparrow on the roof, are its concern also—but augmented by standards of value and shades of feeling, arranged in different dimensions and assigned a quite different focus and perspective. Thus the very same material seems to produce the empirical, the philosophical or the artistic order. The religious life creates the world over again; it interprets the whole of existence in a peculiar key, so that, in keeping with its pure idea, it will not interfere with or contradict world-views built according to other categories—though the life of the individual man may traverse all these strata and become embroiled in their contradictions, because he does not comprehend their totalities but only parts of them.

That is what I mean by the remark at the beginning of this discussion: one element of life, averse to co-operating peacefully with the other ones in life, often takes on a contradictory meaning as soon as it is elevated to an ultimate and absolute status. Only if religion is accepted as the totality of the world-picture, co-ordinated with other theoretical and practical totalities, will it and the other systems of life achieve a harmonious state of inner interdependence.

Limited as he is in his powers and interests, man probably realizes these possible (as it were ideally existing) worlds in harmony to only a small degree. Just as he does not mold all of the immediately given data into scientific knowledge, just as his imaginative powers will not transform all of them into products of art, neither will all of them enter into the aggregate state of religion. For this process of formation, although in principle everywhere within reach, does not always find equally flexible material within all the components of world and spirit. Three segments of life perhaps signify transposition into the religious key: the reaction of man to exterior nature, to his fate and to the surrounding world of man. Our task here is to unfold the last of these: man's relation to his human environment. By linking it with the domain of the two other segments we will discover the contour of a general conception of the religious and its proper place in human relations.

It seems banal to restate that religion is but a mere exaggeration of empirical facts. The world-creating god is seen as a hypertrophy of the causal impulse; we perceive the religious sacrifice as an extension of the known necessity of having to pay a price for everything desired; we experience the fear of God as an accumulation and enlarged reflection of the superpower we meet at every turn in physical nature. But even though this may depict the phenomenon from the outside, it does not make it comprehensible from the inside. To accomplish this, the religious categories must be established actualities and active a priori in the co-operative formation of the material, if this material is to be perceived as religiously important, if religious forms are to be derived from it. Just as the objects of experience are *recognizable*, because the forms and norms of perception have achieved their structure out of the mere material of the senses; just as we are therefore capable of abstracting the law of causality from our experiences, because we have fashioned them accordingly (for only so, after all do they become "experiences") ; so objects are religiously important and raise themselves to transcendental forms because and insofar as they are absorbed by the religious category which determines their formation, before they can be considered as being known and entirely recognized as religious phenomena.

If, indeed, God as the creator of the world originates in the necessary consecutiveness of cause and effect, then the religious element, which aspires to the transcendental, is incorporated from the beginning in the lower strata of the causal process. On the one hand, it remains inside the concrete perception and connects a given link with the next one; but in addition the restless rhythm of this movement causes a degree of dissatisfaction with all the given facts, of the degradation of every single one to infinitesimal nullification in an immeasurable chain—in short, a sound from the religious harmony vibrates a priori in the causal movement. This directed thought, depending on the level on which we let it travel, and on the sentiment which we invest in it, moves toward a world of perceptible nature or toward a point lying in the transcendental. If God is the creative cause of the world, then the inner meaning of this process—being a priori part of a religious category—has been, as it were, crystallized, just as the abstract law of causality indicates that its formula has been extracted from the causal process, insofar as it follows the categories of cognition. The endless succession of causative sequences as the order of an empirically recognizable world would never have culminated in a god; the leap into the religious world could never have been comprehended on the mere strength of these successive causes —had not this very sequence become possible under the shield of the religious feeling as the final expression of the world-creating God, as the substance in which religiosity could coalesce, in the proper meaning of that process.

That our sentimental attachment to surrounding nature can develop under the religious auspice, and that this development confronts itself, as it were, in religion, is much easier to detect. Nature often releases in us feelings of aesthetic well-being, or fear and terror and realization of the grandeur of its superpower—the first by suddenly revealing as transparent and accessible what we thought of as foreign and eternally opposed; the latter by transforming the merely physical, indifferent and intelligible, into a fearful, impenetrable darkness. Then again nature can release in us that radical feeling, so hard to analyze, which I can only define as a stirring of the soul: suddenly we may be deeply touched and moved, not by the extreme beauty or grandeur of natural phenomena, but by a mere ray of the sun vibrating on a leaf, or the swaying of a branch in the wind, or something apparently quite ordinary, which, as if in secret consonance with our innermost being, moves us to passionate agitation.

All these sensations may come to pass without going beyond their immediate competence, i.e., they may be without any religious value; and again they may acquire religious value without changing their content in any way. Sometimes during such sensations we feel a certain tension or elation, a humility or gratitude, as if a manifestation of a soul were speaking to us—all this can only be defined in terms of the religious. It is not yet religion, but it is that event which will turn into religion by continuing to stay in the realm of the transcendental, by converting its very essence into its object and seemingly reacquiring itself through the latter. What has been called the theological proof of God—i.e., the beauty, the form and the order of the world as indicative of a purposely creative absolute power—is but the logical configuration of this religious process. Some sensations aroused by nature are also experienced in the religious category in addition to being experienced in the subjective or aesthetic or metaphysical realm; and just as the empirical object is for us the point of intersection at which a certain number of sensual impressions meet, or into which they are extended, so the object of religion is such a locus in which the aforementioned sentiments find their unity by putting themselves, as it were, beside themselves. And because this point becomes the product of all of these, it seems to oppose to the *individual,* the radiation point of the religious lines, a pre-existing being.

The second sphere which influences the soul religiously is fate. Fate is generally defined as the agency which determines the development of that which man does not represent himself—although his own actions and his own being may be involved in these deciding powers. Because of this meeting of the inner being with something alien to it, the concept of fate contains existentially a motive of chance; which evidences a fundamental tension in the soul with regard to the meaning of life, at even those times when fate acts as the very performer of man's will. Regardless of our attitude toward fate, be it fatalistic or rebellious, hopeful or desperate, demanding or contented, it may be completely irreligious or it may be absolutely religious. However, the religious accent here may not influence the experience as a presumed transcendental power, but must be a particular quality of the emotions themselves, a concentration or a buoyancy, an inspiration or a contrition, which in itself is religious; it creates this object of religion as its objectivation or counterpart, just as the senses create the object which actually confronts them. Even in matters of fate, by definition independent of us, experience in the specific sphere of religion is formed by the productive religious powers; it corresponds to the categories of religious objectivity, because they have formed it by their own effort.

Such is the case, for instance, of "to those who love God, everything will take the most favorable turn." Not exactly in such a manner that the hand of God reaches down from the clouds and arranges things to the best advantage for His dear children, but that the experience of the religious man is a priori thus—that fate is bound to grant him the goods he aspires to in his religious zeal. Whatever course fortune may take on the level of earthly happiness, outward success and intellectual development, in the sphere of religion it is invariably accompanied by such emotional tensions, ordered according to such scales of values, transfigured by such interpretations, that these have to conform with the meaning of religion—the concern of God for the welfare of His children—just as the world, if it is to be apprehended, must develop in a causative mode, because on the level of perception it is formed a priori by this category of causality. Just as perception does not create causality, but causality causes perception, so religion does not condition religiosity, but religiosity begets religion. The experiences man encounters in a certain inner mood stir relations, meanings, sentiments, which of themselves are not yet religion, nor do their realities in any way conform to the religion of a differently attuned soul; but divested of this reality and forming in themselves a sphere of objectivity, they became "religion," which here means "the objectified world of faith."

Finally, let us deal with the relations of man to the world of man as immanent sources of religion. In these relations also, forces and significances become effective independent of religious accentuation by an already existing religion; rather they ascend to it by their own impact. Religion in its ultimate and perfect state, the whole spiritual complex associated with transcendental existence, appears as the absolute, the unified form of emotions and impulses, already developed partially and by trial in social life. To understand this, we will have to analyze the principle of sociological structure, as we did above in regard to the religious principle.

Social life involves the mutual correlation of its elements, which occur in part in instantaneous actions and relations, which partly manifest themselves in tangible forms: in public functions and laws, orders and possessions, languages and means of communication. All such social mutual correlations, however, are caused by distinct interests, ends and impulses. They form, as it were, the matter which realizes itself socially in the "next to each other" and the "with each other," the "for each other" and the "against each other" of individuals. This matter of life may persevere, while a variety of forms absorb it alternately; and vice versa, into the immutable form of the mutual correlation may enter the most varied contents. Thus many norms and results of public life may be aided equally by the free play of competing powers and the regulated custody of lower elements by higher ones. Thus many social interests are preserved for a while by the organization of the family, to be taken over later on or somewhere else by exclusively vocational associations or by governments.

One of the most typical forms of social life, one of those fixed norms by which society secures the proper behavior of its members, is *custom*. (With culturally retarded societies custom is the typical form of socially necessary commissions and omissions.) These same conditions of social life—later codified as law and enforced by the power of the state on the one hand, or left to the discretion of free, cultivated, well-bred men on the other—in narrower and more primitive worlds are guaranteed by that curious and immediate supervision of neighbor by neighbor called custom. Custom, law, unfettered individual morality are different combinations of the social elements, which may, and indeed do, have for their content the same commandments among different peoples and at different periods. These forms by which society determines the proper behavior of the individual include religion. One stage of development in the modes of life is often characterized by a religious tendency. A specific area, which earlier or later is characterized by other forms of relations among men, at a certain period assumes a religious aspect.

This is particularly noticeable with legal processes, which at certain times and in certain places are of the theocratic character, subject wholly to religious sanctions; while under different conditions they may be guaranteed by the power of the state or by custom. Indeed, in many cases the order of society seems to have issued from an entirely undifferentiated form, in which moral, religious or legal sanctions were still one and the same—e.g., the *Dharma* of the Hindus, the *Themis* of the Greeks, the *Fas* of the Romans—and according to different historical circumstances these represent the social order sometimes by one, sometimes by another formative aspect. The frequent retrogression of those regulating norms—from custom to law, from law to custom, from humanitarian obligations to religious sanctions and vice versa—is related to the fact that practical as well as theoretical modes of life turn, in the course of history, from distinctly conscious into unconscious, factual presuppositions and practices, while others—often the same ones—emerge from an unconscious, instinctive state into a clearly intelligible and accountable one. When law instead of custom determines actions, much greater consciousness is involved; unrestrained morality, subject only to one's own conscience, attributes conscious and unconscious intent to the impulses of our actions quite differently than do social regulations. The tension between the darkly motivating emotions and the avowed purposes of action is, in the realm of religious sanctions, much larger than that attributed by custom.

Characteristically, this development of change in the intensity of a relation carries it through a multiplicity of sanctions: during a period of aroused patriotism, e.g., the relations of the individual to his group may acquire a pathos, a dedication, a sincerity, which not only is of itself of a religious character, an act of religiosity, but also resorts far more to the divine power; its impulses integrate themselves much more decidedly into immediate religious agitations than they would during normal times, when these relations are conditioned by convention or the law of the state. Thus it provides at the same time an enhancement of consciousness of the patriotic relation. Such a situation of danger, of passionate agitation, of the triumphs of political homogeneity, which groups the emotions of the individual relative to the situation under a religious aspect and order, generally emphasizes their importance to the individual in a much stronger fashion than during periods when other norms are prevalent. From these norms arises this more pervasive and warmer relation, and into them it will sink back again.

Private relations as well, susceptible to religious sanctions, usually call upon them at the moment when consciousness is most strongly centered on them: e.g., during the ratification of the marriage contract; or during the Middle Ages in the case of all contracts subject to divine approval. The life of the Puritans was marked by an almost abnormally heightened awareness of every aspect of life, by a conscious account-rendering for every act and every thought—for every single part of life was subjected to the religious norm and no other sanction was acknowledged as binding. But here too the opposite holds true: the immense importance of the essentially prehistoric organization of the tribe often fades into a merely religious one with the growing power of the state. True, from the beginning it has been a cultural communion. But apart from the essential requisites of common habitation, common property and mutual protection by law and arms, in the beginning it had to emphasize the awareness of common interests much more than during those epochs when this common weal became merely a community of festivals and sacrificial rites, as was the custom in later Antiquity or in China today. Here the exclusive religious sanctions were matched by a diminished accent on the unity of the group and its significance. The essence of the normative feature was consummated by it, but it explained, as it were, their different mental state of aggregation and their transition as merely formal changes of the same practical contents of life. Wherever these were placed under the protection of religion, religion had to be already in existence. The deciding issue here, however, is not a dogmatic notion in regard to transcendental essences, which form merely the means of sanction, but the fact that the social requirements have attained a degree of stability, an emotional harmony, a consecration, which expresses the degree of necessity for a new social norm.

Whether ordinances for the protection of health, such as were inculcated as divine commands in the ancient Jewish law; whether murder and perjury, which in the seventh and

15

eighth centuries in the territories of German Christianity were punished by the bishop as violations of the divine order; whether obedience to the prince in reverence to his divine rights—everywhere in society modes of life take shape which without their social significance would never have been elevated to religious sanctions. And through this elevation they now develop the energies and forms for which they are attuned by their inner emotional tensions and meanings, which originally had not been borrowed from the transcendental. Never would they have attracted this transcendental norm—as innumerable other norms actually did—had their emotional value, their very unifying powers, their very limitations not led them of their own volition to a projection on the religious level.

II.

The elementary basis by which the religious category is transformed into a social relation is given in the strange analogy existing between the attitude of the individual toward the godhead and social collectivity. Decisive here, above all, is the feeling of dependency. The individual feels himself bound to something universal, something higher, toward which he moves, to which he surrenders, but also from which he expects elation and redemption, feeling different from yet identical with it. God has been characterized as the *coincidentia oppositorum*, the center in which all the antinomies of life are melted, including the extreme multifariousness of the relation of the soul to God and of God to the soul.

Love and estrangement, humility and indulgence, ecstasy and remorse, despair and trust, are not merely shadings in the changing epochs of such a relationship, but each of them leaves an imprint on the basic relation of the soul to its god, so that the soul seems to inhale and exhale with one and the same breath all the antinomies of all possible moods. And the god that is true is just; but he is a forgiving god too, forgiving beyond justice. In the world of Antiquity he stands above all parties, yet taking sides.

17

He is the absolute lord of the world, yet he lets it revolve according to the rigidity of its own laws. While the reciprocal relationship between man and his god thus includes the whole scale of possible relations in "the one after the other" and the "at the same time," it apparently repeats the modes of behavior which regulate the association of the individual with his social group.

Here we find the same encompassment of the individual by a superior power, which nevertheless allows him a certain degree of freedom; a receiving, responded to with a reaction; a surrender not excluding rebellion, a reward and a punishment, the relation of a part to the whole in which the part itself aspires to be a whole. Especially can that humility, in which the pious man confesses—that all he is and all he has he owes to God, and through which he sees in God the source of his being and his power—be transferred to the relation of the individual to society. For in the sight of God man is never a nobody, though he be a mere grain of dust, a feeble perhaps not completely transitory force, a vessel ready to accept that divine gift. Thus both the religious and the sociological forms of individual existence spring from the same source. The latter need only be accompanied by, or blended with, the religious mood to produce the essential form of religion as an autonomous structure or attitude. Without reference to this universal relationship, an expert on the old Semitic religion illustrates it distinctly in the following description: ,

In the period immediately prior to the rise of Islam

the Arabic heroes lacked to a conspicuous degree any religion in the general meaning of the word. They were only perfunctorily concerned with gods and divine subjects and in cultic matters they were completely indolent. On the other hand, they knew a certain religious devotion to the tribe; the life of their own tribesmen was sacrosanct and inviolable. This seeming contradiction becomes plausible, however, in the light of the antique notion by which the god and his followers constitute a community, and the same principle of sanctity applies to the relation of the believers both to each other and to the godhead. The original religious community was the tribe, and all obligations, based on kinship, were at the same time components of the religion, and even when the tribal god had passed from sight and was almost forgotten, the essence of the tribal religion asserted itself in the continued sanctity of the blood relationship.

It can be definitely stated: there exist social conditions, relations among men, of a religious character. They are the same pertinent values which, dissociated from their social aspects and elevated into the transcendental dimension, signify religion in the more precise, autonomous sense. That differentiation of norms which I mentioned before manifests itself historically in even more limited form in the distinction between religious and social obligations. Except for Buddhism and Christianity they are always united. The service of the gods in the entire world of Antiquity and

19

almost everywhere else in the ethnic world, is part of life in the political community or in that of the family, belonging to this life in the same manner as language. To ignore it would be equivalent to the refusal of the duty of bearing arms or to the presumption of creating one's own language. Even Buddhism asserts it, although in a negative form, since it completely lacks the social aspect. The Buddhistic ideal visualizes a monastic life, not excluding occasional sacrifices and sufferings for others, which are not for the sake of others, but only for the ego and the redemption of one's own soul. It teaches absolute withdrawal from the social world. Redemption (*Sich-Erlösen*) for the Buddhist is but a withdrawal (*sich lösen*) from all existence, the social no less than the natural. The Buddhist acknowledges only duties toward himself, and should the welfare of others become involved, then it is "the welfare of all living beings."

This is in sharp contradiction to the political-social demarcation, which defines social obligations in the classical and generally in the non-Christian, world. But then Buddhism is not a religion. It is a teaching about salvation, which anyone can gain entirely through his own efforts, his own volition and his own thinking, and which will automatically be realized if he but meets the conditions existing in, and intrinsic to, the nature of his soul. Deliverance from suffering, as the only substance of Buddhism, does not require a transcendental power to confer grace or act as an intercessor; it is not something *done*, but is a state realized as the logical result of the soul's renouncing all adherence to life. When, therefore, social and religious obligations do not have the correlation they generally display, except for certain differentiations of the Christian culture, the simple explanation is to be found in the lack of this correlation in Buddhism. It simply does not include social norms; it is not religion.

Everywhere else, however—especially among the ancient Semites, Greeks and Romans—the religious obligations of sacrificial offerings, of prayer, of the whole cult, are not a personal concern, but are asked of the individual as a member of a group, and the whole community becomes collectively responsible for the religious trespassing of the individual. That is why, on the other hand, the social life of Antiquity could unfold under the religious aspect; the religious consecration seen superficially as a mere symptom of social necessity, forms in reality an inner, essential and indivisible whole with it. That the social needs are taken under the care of religion, that the relation of the individual to his community is classified as part of one's duties toward God, explains only the prominence of emotional motives, which are already inherent in the social relation.

This backsliding of energies, inherent in the original phenomena and transcending them, is a not uncommon aspect of spiritual life. In a most irrelevant and erroneous manner this is demonstrated by the concept of energy. Between two units of matter a mutual approach takes place; this phenomenon has been explained by the term "power of attraction," which hovers in wondrous vagueness above matter and seems to direct it by invisible arms. However, the concept takes on a more meaningful aspect if the behavior of man in his "milieu" is seen as regulated by "customs." True, it is the immediate and objective significance of such behavior, and its appropriateness to the existence of the group, which endows it with its consecration and its very function as "custom." For the impression that "custom" determines social life as an ideal power, deciding how the particularities of this life are to be conducted, cannot altogether be disregarded. This formal process, however, takes place in the most significant manner wherever it seems to derive its obligations from religion, due to the social appropriateness of the action evolved.

Religion as a product of the soul is indeed nourished from many other sources; its objects release the norms applicable to other spheres of life. Religion is that intersection where all the interests of the soul meet, as soon as they have acquired a certain range of oscillation. We could therefore call it, at the beginning of this discussion, one of those categories or demands which make it possible to blend the totality of life into a specific picture of an all-comprehensive color. If the norms of social bonds appear thus in religious attire, this does not mean they have merely acquired a new label, borrowed from the social facts; it leads them to a general perception, with different content; it joins them with inner energies of a different origin, so that the reflecting sanction is not only a disguise of the existing one; but this sanction, in a new form, is strengthened and enlarged by the others, which flow into and shape the great unity of the religious objects. For even if the content of the transcendental objects is entirely made up of those relations between soul and nature, fate, personal ideas, the soul and individuals, society and mankind, which have their common denominator exclusively in the additive religious frame of mind, through this confluence of the heterogeneous into unities are born entirely new forms. They are more than the mechanical sum of their elements, and their singular meaning cannot be explained by their prorated equation.

I will now discuss specific sociological states and relations which in themselves represent the religious aspect. However, they do not obtain this aspect as the gift or demand of a prevalent religion, but reversely: they themselves will contribute to religion by their autonomous religious values. With their help the basic religious mood acquires a certain form, whose transcendental gradation and objectivation unfold the objects of religion in their general meaning. These in turn, it is true, may invest them with a new consecration and strength.

The relation of a devoted child to his parents, of an ardent patriot to his fatherland or a similarly enthusiastic cosmopolitan to mankind; the relation of a worker to his class, which is pressing onward, or of a nobleman conscious of his rank to the aristocracy; the relation of the vanquished to his conqueror, or of the good soldier to his army—all these relations with their infinitely manifold contents can indeed have a general tenor as far as their psychic aspect is concerned—which must be called a religious key. They all are informed by a strange mixture of selfless devotion and desire, of humility and elation, of sensual immediacy and spiritual abstraction, not only in alternating moods, but in a persistent unity, which can only be comprehended through this division into opposing pairs. Placing a subject in a higher order produces in the individual a particular degree of emotional tension, a specific tenderness and firmness of the inner relation, which he recognizes as belonging to him personally and intrinsically.

These emotional elements, which form, at least in part, both the inner and the outer side of such relations, we call religious elements. For the very fact that they are religious gives them a flavor distinguishing them from relations based on sheer egoism or pure suggestion or mere outward or even moral powers. This particular emotional frame of mind can perhaps, generally speaking, be defined as *piety*. Piety is an emotion of the soul which turns into religion whenever it projects itself into specific forms. Here it should be noted that *pietas* means the pious attitude towards both man and God. Piety, which is religiosity in a quasi-fluid state, will not necessarily have to coalesce into a stable form of behavior vis-à-vis the gods, i.e., into religion. Moods or functions which according to their very logic point, as it were, beyond the soul, remain in its sphere, and they will hold good in any object. There exist souls whose very being and action are steeped in the characteristic gentleness, warmth and devotion of love, who yet never feel love for a particular individual. There exist evil hearts whose very thought and longing runs the whole gamut of a cruel and selfish mind, without actually crystallizing into evil deeds. There live artistic natures whose functional capacity to visualize things, to experience life, and to form their impressions and feelings is of an absolutely artistic quality, but who never produce a work of art. There live pious men who do not turn their piety toward any god, i.e., to that phenomenon which is the very object of piety; they are religious natures without a religion. They belong among those human beings who experience and feel the previously described states in a religious frame of mind. We call it "religious" because the autonomous object, which sprang from it of itself, exists as an object of the religion in existence, as the bacilli culture of impulses, moods and needs which grow under those conditions out of the empirical, social matter.

One might assume that the sociological relations thus psychologically characterized were genuine religious phenomena. One might take it for granted that these functions which establish themselves independently and increase in social substance beyond their approved extent, would create "gods" as their objects. We know of many analogies, relating to seemingly very heterogeneous phenomena. We have often observed how the love impulse creates its own objects, not by merely searching for an adequate object which will serve its pleasures, transferring to this object those longed-for values which are missing in reality; but as the object of love the loved one is always a creation of the lover. Love creates a new form—related, it is true, to a real person, but existing essentially and ideally in a completely different world, which does not enter into the reality of this human being. One should not mistake the imagined qualities of the contents for the quest for form or essence, which is our subject matter here. The image of the beloved one emerging from those qualities may or may not correspond to reality; the productivity of the lover, creating the beloved as a configuration beyond all other materializations of things, becomes neither superfluous on that account, nor is it substantiated. It is as with a work of art, which, in contradistinction to any mere imitation of nature, has a creative meaning, regardless of its having taken its substance from a given reality. A work of art wells up from the productive inner emotion of the artist. It is art when and insofar as this emotion has manifested itself in an object of art. It represents therefore, something much more than and quite different from the marble block, in which form it existed in the world of tangible reality—something quite different, too, as a form abstracted from the world of experience. Thus the human being loved by his fellow represents a totally new category of being. He is the seed of love, regardless of whether the qualities he possesses in the eyes of the lover correspond to his other reality or are pure fantasy.

With this hint, the self-evident cliché that the gods are the outgrowth of the religious frame of mind is placed in a wider and, in my opinion, not so self-evident context. The efficaciousness of certain fundamental powers and impulses of the soul means that they produce an object for themselves. The significance of the object of these functions of love, of art, of religiosity, is merely the significance of these functions as such. Each of them places its object in its own world, thereby begetting this object as its own. And it does not matter whether the elements which come together in this particular form are already in existence or not: they become now a new form in its own right. When the religious impulse admits these sociological facts, when the relation of the individual to individuals of a higher order or to a social entity or its ideal norms or symbols, in which a grouping assumes the accent we call religious, then functionally this is seen as the same act of creation of his soul as it is with "religion." He has populated the world of his religious impulses just as if he were praying to a god; but with the prayer the function seems to remain more self-contained, because it has not absorbed any matter already predetermined.

But that is unimportant for the principle we are trying to elaborate here. The objects of religiosity man finds in certain social relations are products of his piety. Whether relations of this order came first historically, coalescing with the transcendental by the abstraction and sublimation of the religious element of the emotions; or whether they relate to a being with self-denying sentiments and tendencies, free-moving and purely functional; or whether they have procured for themselves an object serving their ends regardless of their effect on their fellow men and social institutions—all this must remain here (and probably always) undetermined. The understanding we seek here is not of a historical, chronological sequence, but of the absolutely factual: we are trying to prove that the religious world has its roots in the spiritual complexity of the relation of the individual to his fellow man or to a group of his fellow men, as in the purer phenomena of religion (in the conventional meaning of the word).

27

III.

If I now try to examine the analogies between social and religious behavior in their particular contours, it will become apparent that I mean by analogy not an accidental equality of phenomena, independent of each other, but unity of a psychical category, expressing itself sometimes in the material of human reciprocity, which substantiates—not transforming but directly forming—these very impulses in purely autochthonous forms. The immanence of the one and the transcendence of the other phenomena are merely differentiations of matter—and, as it were, its arrangement—to which the fundamental function of religion resorts.

I turn first to *faith*, usually understood as the essential and specific expression of religion, as its substance. In our terminology faith will have to be distinguished from what is commonly called "faith" in the theoretical meaning of the word. In its intellectual meaning it belongs in the same rank with knowledge, being a lower degree of it. It is an "assuming to be true" for reasons that are quantitatively inferior to those which, as we claim, are the basis of our knowledge. Thus metaphysical investigations or those of the theory of perception may lead us to consider the existence of God as a plausible or, under certain circumstances, even necessary hypothesis. That means, to believe in God in the same way as one accepts the existence of light or the atomistic structure of matter. But we sense immediately that the religious man who says, "I believe in God," means something additional to a mere attestation to the existence of God. This existence, it is alleged, although not provable, is nevertheless considered a fact. It means also a positive inner relation to God, an emotional devotion to Him, a direction of life toward Him. The conviction of one's own existence as part of any other reality is only one aspect of, or one theoretical expression of, that physical and subjective being which is in effect meant with the sentence: "I believe in God." This propensity of the religious soul, affirmed by this sentence, is the fountain of youth by which theoretical faith in the existence of God always reasserts itself in defiance of all counterevidence and counterprobabilities.

A curious interpretation of this meaning of "faith" is revealed in the fact that there exists a relation among men which is expressed by the same term: we "have faith in" someone. This surely is not intended to indicate that we believe in his existence; on the other hand, it does not define exactly what we do believe with regard to the other person. "Believing in someone" denotes a basic, specific, psychological fact: the child believes in his parents, the subaltern in his superior, the friend in his friend, the lover in his beloved, the subject in his prince. Belief in the reality of certain qualities in objects of our faith is a consequence of the fundamental relation, indicating a certain bent of the whole human being in regard to the other one. Moving on a level beyond proof or refutation, such faith in a person survives the most substantiated suspicions, and clear evidence of the unworthiness of the one we believe in. This is the *religious* faith, manifesting itself in the relation of man to man. Faith in God is just this competence, abstracted from the subject, freed from its empirical object and its relative dimensions, producing its object from its own resources and therefore elevating it into the absolute. The sociological and transcendental forms of this faith produce, for the subject himself, first of all, analogous results.

It has justly been stressed how much strength and tranquillity, how much moral reliability and what relief from the toils of a weary life, faith in a divinity contributes to the well-being of man, quite independent of its objective reality. For faith is a condition of the soul, relating to something beyond it, yet possessing this relation as an inner, intrinsic attribute. The soul, indeed, draws these elation-generating forces out of its own depth, but by letting them pass the stations of the faith in God, it gains a more concentrated and productive form, it confronts its forces with themselves and thus, reincorporating them into itself, it can modify them into otherwise unattainable modes of value. This strangely effectual arrangement, whereby faith acts upon the psychical energies, can also be brought about by applying this faith to the relations of man to man.

Faith in a human being, even though it be objectively unjustified, has the immense advantage of kindling many

31

things in our soul and uniting passing events which otherwise would have remained unconscious or ineffective. A man cheers us up with trivial arguments, but we want to believe he is giving us the best and the right advice, and so he liberates in our soul latent, alleviating resources. He supports us in our suffering with inadequate and improper palliatives, but trusting his help we take new courage and strength. He tries to prove something to us by way of a poor argument, and in accepting it as true we discover for ourselves the correct answer. Very often do we confer on someone in whom we trust, those treasures which are our very own; yet he has inspired us to dig into ourselves for these treasures. What it all comes to is the belief of man in himself. This faith as self-confidence demonstrates that all its separate components are merely the forms by which single causes realize a basic spiritual frame of mind. Our faith in a person or in God indicates that anxiety and insecurity as expressions of our common fate have been alleviated: the image of these phenomena is a sedative for the turbulence of the soul, and the fact that we "depend on them" in a particular case is a projecting of this feeling of security which characterizes our mental condition under the influence of its image.

The same importance accrues to faith in ourselves: it is tranquillity and certainty grounded in an ultimate concept of the ego, conditioned by the notion that this ego will victoriously survive and overcome every adverse situation. Due to this identical basic psychical behavior, faith in God and belief in oneself often give man the same serene imperturbability, the same confidence in the future, the same easy substitution of a new hope for a value just proven fallacious. And regardless of how often it may lead us astray and how costly may be this self-assurance, this anticipation of our accomplishments, faith in oneself has the same efficacy as faith in others. How many things are we capable of accomplishing because we believe that we can do them; how often is a talent pressed to its ultimate limit because we assume this boundary line to be still farther away. A man may act meritoriously from a sense of *noblesse oblige*, although his character does not warrant such behavior; it is his belief in these noble qualities which brings them to the fore.

Practical faith is a basic, essentially sociological attitude of the soul, i.e., it becomes active in relation to a being confronting the ego. Man can accomplish this even with regard to himself, for he is capable of splitting himself into a subject and an object, of confronting himself as if he were a third person—a faculty, as far as we know, without analogy among the other creatures of this world —and this ability is the foundation of our entire rational nature. Faith in the ego, in another one, and in God proves so frequently alike because all the manifestations are expressions of the same spiritual tensions, differing only according to the sociological object.

So far nobody has inquired beyond the individual meaning of this religious faith, into its purely social significance; but I am sure that without it society as we know it could not exist. Our unswerving faith in a human being or a collective beyond all proof, often against all proof, is one of the strong bonds by which society is held together. Submissive obedience is very often not based on positive knowledge of the right and superiority of the other one, nor is it rooted in love and suggestion, but rather in that "faith" in the power, the merit, the irresistibility and goodness of the other one—a faith which is not merely a theoretical hypothesis, but a very particular spiritual phenomenon operating among men. And neither will this faith spend itself in those particular qualities it imagines as the values of its objects; for they are relatively accidental subject matters, by which faith substantiates itself in its formal disposition and tendency and becomes manifest and articulate.

Faith as a sociological power, therefore, joins with many different, related powers—be it those of knowledge, of the will or of the emotions—while in its pure form, operating by itself, it represents faith in God—an absoluteness which reveals its very nature in those low and mixed phenomena. In this faith in God the process of "believing in someone" has dissociated itself from the ties which bound it to the social counterpart; it has procreated its object from its own resources even in respect to its contents, while it has discovered in its social efficacy an object already given in other orders. But this faith does not merely become religious by extending into the transcendental, which is just its dimension and mode of representation; it is already religion in its sociological form. By its synthesis of constraint and expansion of the ego, of sagacity and blindness, of spontaneity and dependency, of giving and receiving—all of which are part of it—it forms a section of the religious level, to which the mutual relations of men are projected and which borrows the name and its popular concept, but never its essence exclusively from the characteristic transcendental forms, which reveal indeed their structure most distinctly in it.

It could be said: God is the very object of faith. In God the faithful crystallize the basic strength of this function without distraction and isolation. From this origin, from the totality and originality of the psychical energy, as far as it is still to be found beyond its singular and therefore always relative applications, is derived the character of the *absolute* in the conception of God. And thereby the function of faith ranks equally with a number of other psychical operations, which allow only their most general, undifferentiated, prejudiced energy to enter into the religious substance. Thus the God of Christianity is the very object of love. All those particular qualities of men and things, by which this very precise quality allows us to realize our potentialities of love for them, give to love a particular aspect, so that love for someone else, as it were, finds itself as a different, separate case of the same general concept: to love someone else is a different love. Love thus becomes an empirical object, notwithstanding the fact that it remains of course an act in the lover, but a product derived, as it were, from *his* energy and the quality of its object. But because the soul cannot conceive God empirically, since God does not confront man as a differentiated individuality, He becomes the abstract product of the very energies of love, whose ramifications, which usually realize

35

themselves in individual objects, remain undivided.

In the same sense God is also the object of search as such. The restlessness of the inner life, constantly altering the objects of mental images, here finds its absolute object; a particular object is no longer sought—which always means a particular search—but the search finds its goal in God. This corresponds to the undercurrent of searching, of the "gone, gone," of the unrest, by which all particular yearning for a change becomes just a phenomenon or a part. When God is "the end as such," He is indeed the end of the search as such. Thus is demonstrated, too, the deeper meaning of His origin as the absolute causal impulse (*Verabsolutierung des Kausaltriebes*). In the realm of the empirical this impulse exists always as a particular object of an individual aspect, in which a specific matter and the causal form have grown together into a unity. But insofar as the causal impulse becomes effective without such particular stimulation and does not absorb a singular substance, but produces its object as a pure function, this object becomes the absolute universality, and the cause of existence is the only object of the causal impulse as an undifferentiated energy. In characterizing God as the *ens perfectissimum*, as beyond all limitation and particularity, Scholasticism objectifies the divine image from what we may call the absolute in *our soul*: from its pure, self-propelled functions, which are not specialized by a singular object caused by these functions.

To define God as "love as such," therefore, means only to apply this quality to the subject as it has passed into that state. God is not an individual object of love, but he originates (although this notion will not be realized without difficulty) in the impulse of love in its purest form, in the absolute state of love beyond its relative states, i.e., reduced to relativity by individual objects. Thus is defined His psychological relation to society-forming occurrences among men. All functions, e.g., love and faith, longing and devotion, tie the subject which harbors such emotions to other subjects; the network of society is knit together by these innumerable differentiations; they are, as it were, the a priori forms which as individual suggestions make up empiric, social-psychic individualities. When they become effective in their pure originality, freed from limitations by a counterpart, the absolute, the religious object becomes their goal and product. In the objective religious idea, the individual events of reality relate to the divine being as their absolute, undivided source, uniting its disjunctive attributes; and the manifold individualized impulses, sociologically uniting the souls, relate psychologically to the effective basic impulse, representing the general in regard to these schisms, each in its own language placing the absolute of man in religious relation to the absolute of existence.

A second concept in which social and religious phenomena reveal an identity of form—so that the social form approximates the religious aspect, while the religious presents itself as the symbol and the absolute of the social form—is unity. The confusing multitude of things, from which here and there emerges a causally related pair of phenomena, gives to more primitive epochs only *one* opportunity to experience multiplicity as unity, i.e., the social group. Its consciousness of unity will unfold from a twofold antithesis, and to begin with from the hostile demarcation dividing it from other groups. Common defense and attack against a competitor for living space is one of the powerful means of realizing the togetherness of the elements of the group and impressing it on them. This unity very often comes about—or at least becomes conscious—not from inside but by outside pressure, through the practical exigency of this form of existence, and also in a large degree through the practical example of external powers, which show the complexity of existence to be indeed homogeneous. Furthermore, it is the attitude of the group to its individual elements which characterizes it as a unity. Exactly because they are separate, and thus mobile, exactly because they are to a certain extent free and responsible only to themselves, the outcome of their coalescence will be perceived as a unity. Exactly because the individual feels that he is an individual, the uniting power which welds him to others will become more marked; since in his devotion to this harmony he feels the totality of life penetrate his being, and in opposition to it he sees himself as an adversary to the whole.

That the spirit of freedom of the individual tries to shirk the unity of the whole, that this unity will not be carried through as spontaneously with even the narrowest and most naïve structure, as is the case with the unity of an organism in its parts—exactly this fact makes it apparent that the uniting force is a specific form or energy of existence. The frequent organization of primitive hordes in groups of ten is a clear indication that the ratio of the elements of the group corresponds to that of the fingers: in relative freedom and independent mobility, the individual nevertheless joins others in a union of concerted action and indivisible existence. All social life is based on reciprocity and that means unity. For what is unity if not the mutual union of the many and the correlative effect of the fate of every element of the group upon all the others?

The synthesis in the group is the prototype of the perceived, the conscious unity, transcending personality, and its particular form is mirrored or sublimated in the religious unity of existence, held together by the concept of God. An inquiry into the religious grouping will elucidate this relationship. It is well known that in primitive civilizations (including so-called uncivilized ones) groupings of a permanent or organic type exist only as cult communities. During the period of the Roman emperors a strong trade unionism brought forth innumerable guilds and each of them seems to have had its own characteristic religious cachet. Regardless of whether these guilds were formed by merchants or actors, stretcher bearers or physicians, they placed themselves under the protection of a particular deity or they had their *genius loci;* they owned a temple or at least an altar. Not the individual member but the group stood under the protection of a specific god; thus it was the *unity* of the group, represented by this god, which kept them together and transcended the individual. The deity was, as it were, the name for the sociological unity; because insofar as it was sensed *sub specie religionis* it called forth the specific reaction of devoutness.

No less important is the role this sociological unity played in early Christianity. Its importance increased more and more until it overshadowed true religious values. During the third century there arose a violent controversy whether Christians who had left the fold during the times of persecutions should be readmitted. The Bishop of Rome was in favor of their reinstatement; thereupon the more orthodox party elected a new, equally qualified bishop. Nor was there any doubt that the religious consequences, the inner purity of the Church, justified excluding the apostates or at least allowing the more rigorous adherents to stay to themselves. But Cyprian saw to it that the election of the counterbishop was declared void, because *unity* was felt to be absolutely vital to the interest of the Church.

Christianity had inherited this form of unity from the spirit of the guilds, especially predominant during the later period of the Roman Empire. The first and original unity among Christians in their communion of love, faith and hope was actually more a "next to each other" of sympathetic souls than an organic "with each other"; the latter form they borrowed from the surrounding world of the pagans, although in Christianity it acquired a hitherto unknown power and profundity. And during the decline of the antique world, because of this firm sociological structure the Church acquired the value of an absolute; it became a refuge provided by the transcendental, indeed a manifestation of the immediate divine. The Christian dogma of redemption as such does not oppose the coexistence of several sociologically independent communities, kept together merely by the same doctrines and ideals. The vigor of this loyalty, however, was very soon found lacking, unless it was organized and brought into a sociological unity—not merely as a technical method of guaranteeing the stability and external power of the new religion, but as the mythical reality of salvation itself. By virtue of its all-embracing form of unity the Church seemed to be the realization of the Kingdom of God, as it had been foretold by Jesus. It was praised as the "City of God," as Noah's Ark, harboring in its walls the holy community of saved souls; it is the "Body of Christ." The process these pages are trying to make intelligible is perhaps nowhere else so plainly evident. The purely empirical-sociological form of unity, historically developed, is appropriated by the religious feelings and thus reveals itself as the counterpart or the mythical reality of the transcendental undividedness of the purely religious unification (*Zusammengefasstsein*) of the world. The specific value of religion becomes evident here as the ideal expression of the sociological form of reciprocity which we call the unity of the group.

One specific trait of this group unity is particularly conducive to religious development. The molding of the group into a unity, especially during more primitive epochs, is marked by the absence of struggles and competition among its members in contrast to its relation to the outside world. This form of existence of the unrivaled "next to each other," the concordance of goals and interests, presents itself nowhere else so clearly and completely as in the religious sphere, and the peaceful coexistence of the ordinary group life resembles a rather preliminary stage. For the preliminary stage is but relative; in empirical society the members still tend to remain rivals for the same goal, to improve the discongruity between desires and gratification even at the expense of others; to say the least, they try to find in their disparity with others a standard of values for personal actions and amenities. It is mainly on the religious level that the energies of the individual will completely attain their ends without coming into conflict with each other, because, according to the beautiful saying of Jesus, in the house of God there is room for everyone. They all strive, it is true, for the same end, but each man has the opportunity to reach this goal without interference from a rival, indeed through an expressly co-operative effort.

Let us bear in mind how profoundly communion expresses religion's aim of realizing equal ends for all through equal means. I call especially to mind the festivals which display the unity of all participants in an identity of religious inspiration, from the crude festivals of primitive religions, where the all-embracing unity is usually climaxed by sexual orgies to the purest call of the *pax hominibus*, transcending all individual groups. The Christian festival of Christmas is primarily a universalistic expression of the communion of peace, which in particular religions finds its symbols in the community of individual groups. For in the community of the group the conciliation of enmity is realized only so far as its uniform mode of life depends on it—i.e., only partially and relatively. The group-directed religion clears the ground for internal peace, unhampered by such limitations, which finds its expression in the festivals. The Christian festivals, and perhaps most manifestly Christmas, heighten this motive of peace; they present themselves to the individual as moments of elation, when together with all Christianity he is borne by his emotions into a communion which will overcome all special partisan antagonisms.

Such a condition we must concede, is very imperfectly substantiated in historical reality. As to its *import*: the Christian festival realizes a very unique social-psychological fact; it radically lifts the barriers which usually separate the individual spiritually from the strangeness of contrary sympathies. The social principle of conciliation thus transcends that sociologically inward character and the spirit of these religious festivals gains a positive and universalistic symbol. Both the Jewish and the early Christian communities saw to it that all conflicts between their members were settled by the community or by communally appointed arbitrators. Paulus pointed out the incompatibility of submitting to judges who were despised heathens.

As to pacification, the religious community represents here an increment of the inner unity of the group; religion is, as it were, peace in substance, that form of a crystallized idea of group life which we call peaceableness. The believers might collide as private persons, as competitors in the economic field, as evildoers—but for recipients of the same religious goods there could only be peace, and the community became therefore the social manifestation of these goods. It was, so to speak, the logically indicated instance which peacefully dissolved all conflicts. The unification and reconciliation by which religion illumines the world-picture is symbolized by the fact that the peace within, to some extent pervading every group, culminates in the religious group. It becomes, as it were, the transfiguration by which the sociological uniformity becomes the absolute unity of the God idea.

This scale has still another rung, characterizing in many respects the pre-Christian epochs. Here the divinity does not face, so to speak, the individual and his circles, but is included in this orbit; the god is an element of the totality of life on which the individual depends. In ancient Judaism, e.g., the god participated at the occasion of the burnt offering; the sacrifice was not merely the payment of a tribute. Everywhere there existed a kin relationship between the god and his worshipers. And everywhere he is regarded as the progenitor of the tribe, its king, the god of this very tribe or this very town—while other gods, whose existence is never doubted, are owned by other groups. In all these instances the god is the supreme *member* of the community. He lives within the social unity and represents at the same time its symbol. As such he faces the individual, but as the *pater familias*, as the representative of the family, or as the prince represents the totality of his subjects. The strangely complicated sociological status of these elements as members of a circle, comprising all the members of the group in a unity, and yet facing them, in a sense, as an independent and counterbalancing power—that is the aspect of the godhead. The god therefore exemplifies that characteristic which marks in this sense the corresponding form of the society. While the Semitic community rested on the kinship of the tribe, the god was for the Jews, the Phoenicians and Canaanites a father, and the worshipers were his children. Wherever, however, the community grew into a political association of several tribes, the god inevitably acquired the characteristics of a king. Removed and less accessible, he now symbolized a much more abstract type of the whole. Stepping out of the narrow circle of the tribal communion, he became, in a technical sense, a "super"-structure.

But even if the "super" is emphasized, the vital relation to the form of the group was not severed. In Greece and Rome the monarchy was early displaced by an aristocracy, and an aristocratic constitution of the religious was established as a multiplicity of gods, all enjoying the same privileges. It is a pure, abstract symbol of mere form, in which the communion of the group is living, removed from the interference of economic, tribal or political interests. In Asia, however, where the monarchy maintained itself much longer, the mode of religion tended toward a monarchic dominance of the god. Indeed the mere strength of the tribal union, dominating the social life of the ancient Arabs, by its very characteristics preformed monotheism. And the very unification, transcending the differentiation of the sexes, forms a specific religious type. The psychological haziness of the difference of the sexes, which played such an important role in the social life of the Syrians, Assyrians and Lydians, is consummated in the concept of their deities, who embody these contrasts: e.g., the half-male Astarte, the male-female Sandon, the sun god Melkarth, who interchanges sex symbols with the moon goddess.

We do not mean to stress the platitude that man portrays himself in his gods—a trite truth not to be accentuated. Rather we will have to acknowledge that not only do the gods represent an idealization of individual qualities: e.g., the strength, the moral as well as immoral characteristics, the tastes and needs of individuals; but the interindividual forms of social life often signify the religious concepts. As the mode of the unity, in the concept of which the reciprocal effect of the elements is comprised, transmigrates into the religious province of the soul, causing a religious reaction, it parts from life, which operates according to its social contents. The transcendental world is the locus where this religiously sensed form crystallizes into objects, just as the three-dimensional sphere of perception is the locus where the sensually perceived becomes an object.

IV.

The above-accentuated relation of standing simultaneously inside and outside of society applies both to the prince and each of its members; and the basic sociological form pre- forms the god as well as the believers. We have already mentioned that the structural membership of the individual in his group always means some mixture of enforced limita- tion and personal freedom. This will be revealed as the most profound form relation between social and religious life.

The real, practical problem of society arises from its inherent powers and forms in relation to the individual lives of its members. It is true that society lives only through individuals. But that does not exclude a multiplicity of an- tagonisms and conflicts. For on the one hand, the individuals form this society out of elements which crystallize into this particular form of "society"; society in turn evokes its own representatives and organs, confronting the individual with demands and orders as if it were an extraneous party. On the other hand, conflict accrues from the invasions of the individual by society. For man's faculty of splitting himself into parts and then experiencing a particular part as his very ego, which collides with other parts and struggles to make a decision to act—this faculty of man often puts him,

47

insofar as he is a social being and so recognizes himself, into an antagonistic relation with the impulses and interests of his ego which are not part of his social character. The conflict between individual and society is transposed in the individual himself into a struggle between the antinomies of his nature.

I see the most capacious and far-reaching collision between society and individual, not in the aspect of particular interests but in the general form of the individual life. Society aspires to totality and organic unity, each of its members constituting but a component part. The individual as part of the society has to fulfill special functions and employ all his strength; he is expected to modify his skills so that he will become the best-qualified performer of these functions. But this role is opposed by man's bent toward unity and totality as an expression of his own individuality. He strives for his own perfection rather than for a model society; he wants to develop his faculties in their totality without concern for the special requirements demanded of him in the interest of society. This is truly the essential meaning of the individualistic demands of liberty over against social restrictions. For the meaning of liberty is not the realization of something arbitrary, independent of social determination. Liberty means absolute self-responsibility, which we own only insofar as our particular actions are the very expression of our personality, insofar as our ego, not prejudicated by any exterior power, finds in these actions its own significance. We wish the periphery of our existence to be determined by forces at its center and not by external powers in which it is entangled, and which, it is true, transform themselves in us into inward personal impulses. But only too often do we sense that they do not originate in the ego at all. The freedom of the individual, which makes him truly responsible for his deeds, means that in all his actions he is a coherent, organic whole, which opposes the claim of a superior entity to subject and rule him as a subordinated part.

If the longing for liberty thus fights subordination to social powers as one pretension opposing another, in the religious sphere this problem seems to shift from a question of law into one of facts. It is a question imbedded in the depth of all religion, although it may remain undeveloped and unconscious, latent and fragmentary: Does the divine will, as the absolute sovereign over the processes of the universe, determine man in such a fashion that man has neither freedom nor responsibility—or has God given us autonomy of soul, which grants both freedom and responsibility, but separates us from full expression of them by divine will (although this is really an incongruous concept)?

Only an apparent answer can be given by logical deliberation or deduction from revelation: in reality it is man's *longing* to be independent even from the highest power and to discover the meaning of his life by his own efforts—and here he collides with his other desire, to be part of the divine world order, and to secure from its grandeur and beauty some value for himself which he can gain only by selfless devotion and subordination. The dignity of individual liberty, and the strength or defiance of self-responsibility which

49

dares to bear all the consequences of sin, collide with the exoneration of the ego by divine superior power, with the easy or even ecstatic abandonment to the knowledge of being part of an absolute entity, and unconditionally possessed by its powers and its meaning. The ego's consciousness obviously confronts here the same problem in regard to both religious and social questions. They are only two forms and expressions of a dualism, defining our souls and our fate at their ultimate root.

From a purely conceptual point of view a solution of this problem seems quite possible: it is a structure of the whole, founded on the very independence and complete unity of its elements, and perfected only in this unity. The controversy therefore would not be a logical one, where the different sides exclude each other a priori, but a mere factual one, which can be solved by the transformation of the elements without changing them in their essence; as to the sociological case, this is at least imaginable as the ideal condition, approximated by the factual ones in the infinite. The perfect society would be the one which is composed of perfect individuals.

Society lives a life of its own in a particular combination of abstractness and concreteness, and each individual contributes to it certain of his characteristics and strength; society grows through the contributions of the individuals, who—beyond it—form or try to form their existence as individualities. On the other hand, this supra-individual, total structure might be organized in such a way that it would receive the most advantageous contributions from those very individuals who are in unison with themselves, whose lives center harmoniously in themselves. Then perhaps the individuality of the whole, transcending the individuals and causing by this division and autonomy a conflict between *its* form and those of individual existences, might again descend to the latter. The fact that the state or any other social organization forms its own conditions and developments of life—as it were, on an abstract level and unconcerned about the individual life of its members, forcing them into services and pressing them into forms of existence which do not conform at all with the laws of their personal beings—this fact may have an abstract grandeur, but then again it may be only a precursory prelude, making a virtue out of necessity.

Compared with this, it might seem utopian, though not unthinkable, that a complete, uniform totality of social elements should evolve elements which are well proportioned, contented existences, growing harmoniously in their peculiar atmosphere. In the subspiritual world this seems contradictory: no house can consist of houses, no tree can consist of trees. But if in organic nature this contradiction is partly mitigated—for the cell of an organism leads a kind of independent life somewhat analogous to the life of the whole—so the soul might be capable, at least in principle, of accomplishing the otherwise impossible: of being simultaneously a whole and part of a whole, helping to form in completely individual freedom a superindividual order.

For the religious order, however, this scheme does not apply. Society is interested ultimately only in the substantially clear-cut qualities and actions of its members, and insofar as they serve the unity and perfection of its existence, society will not object if they also yield for the subject himself a free, harmonious, full life. In respect to God, however, the particular purports are no longer important. It no longer matters whether we act in agreement or in opposition to His will; what is at stake here is the principle of freedom, independence as such and in its most profound sense. The question here is: Is man indeed responsible for his actions, or does God act through him as through a selfless organ? Is a self-centered will ever to be justified as a final end—even though it may not differ in its objects from the divine command? Or is not co-ordination with the divine order of the world, which might well harmonize substantially with the self-fulfillment of the individual, the only motive of life? And is not life, therefore, largely denied any culminating formation, any organization in an autonomous form? Revelation represents here, too, as a condition in the religious order, enhancement and absolution in the social order. The conflict between the whole and the part, which wants to be a whole itself, between the freedom of the elements and their being encompassed by a higher unity in the social sphere is ultimately only cursory and, so to speak, only technically unsolvable. For the divine, world-redeeming essence it becomes, however, a principal, spiritual and by its roots an irreconcilable contradiction.

A special aspect of this tension between the uniting and antagonistic elements, between the part and the whole, discloses—notwithstanding external differences—the same role of the religious essence as against the social one. In accordance with its development society presses its members into a division of labor. The more diversified their work becomes, the more they depend on each other, the stronger becomes the uniformity arising from the exchange of products, the reciprocal effect in the gratification of their interests, the supplementing of their personal characteristics. The justification for regarding an organism's unity of life as a symbol of society derives from the division of labor—in a most general, not merely an economic sense. It is based on the particular functions of the elements by which they are interlinked: one taking the place which the other does not fill, one being concerned with the needs of the others, while the others take care of *his* needs.

Division of labor is the corrective to competition. The latter is an antagonistic displacement of individuals, because they compete for the same ends, leaving no room for mutual co-operation; division of labor, however, is a mutual yielding and simultaneous supplementing, because each chooses a field and settles an area which has not yet been occupied by others. Division of labor helps to accomplish social unity to the same degree as competition tends to destroy it. But the full scope and the more specialized development it grants the individual threatens to turn into contraction and curtailment, if it comes into contact with the antagonistic principle of competition, as has been happening ever more frequently in modern civilization. For the division of labor is predominantly but a differentiation of means and ways to an end, besetting all those who toil: the favor of the public,

53

participation in the available goods and gratifications, the acquisition of superior position, of power and glory. These most general values fall prey to competition.

As a rule division of labor will not definitely supplant competition by new and ultimate ends, but only divert it by momentary digressions. The increasing density of the population, and the needs each newly established particular accomplishment elicits, bring forth furthermore a new multitude of competitors, and exactly that point where competition should be dispelled becomes a new center of conflict. And the play starts here all over again, i.e., the intensity of competition brings forth an always more differentiated division of labor. It leads to the specialization of the individual, the exclusiveness of specialist activity, the curtailment of all energies which do not serve this purpose—to the detriment of all very complicated civilizations. And this is the very cause of the above-described conditions: the interests and the life of society press the individual into a partial existence, which is entirely incompatible with the ideal of his personality, i.e., the forming of a harmonious, well-rounded perfection of being. By endlessly increasing competition, division of labor in its culmination unveils itself as that form which is entirely adequate to the interwoven texture and organic unity of society and the gratification of its needs; but it obtains this perfection at the cost of the imperfection of the individual, as it forces his faculties into specific activities against his nature, thus thwarting innumerable potentialities of these faculties.

The religious plane reflects these modes of behavior of

the individual in respect to the higher totality in special angles of refraction. Religion in its most profound meaning, as the road to the soul's salvation, offers an equality which envelops all souls; it becomes the immediate bond of each soul with the absolute. This union, this communion, originates in this equality rather than in a differentiation which will be accomplished by a common goal as a mutual supplement. Where a multitude of believers "cries to God," the mere physical concentration of prayers, as it were, has its effect as long as both worshipers and their God stay in immediate relationship. This common prayer is not one of many possible communications with the god, a new avenue to his ear, but merely a summation, which by its accretion might impress God more deeply than the lingering voice of the individual. This type of religious relation rejects on principle any differentiation. The perfection of the whole does not depend, as does the above-mentioned social phenomenon, on the varied activities, but on the congenial activities, of the individual. The perfection of the one does not call for completion of the other. For the very communion of the believers here rests truly in the divine itself, that is to say insofar as each individual pays homage to it and is accepted by it.

Here I intend to concentrate on one particular aspect of one phenomenon of the division of labor in the religious sphere: i.e., the priesthood. Buddhism recognizes most distinctly the sociological origin of priesthood. It claims the religious functions, originally performed by each individual, have passed on to specific persons who perform these

55

duties in behalf of the others—just as the monarchy apparently came about when men who originally took personal revenge for the wrongs they suffered elected a representative for the express purpose of punishing evildoers, and rewarded him in return with a share of their harvest. In the priesthood as a labor-dividing agent, religion also attained a singular sublimation, an abstract synthesis of the formative power of practical social phenomena. Here the division of labor is characterized by two motives: on the one hand, there is the difference in personal abilities, qualifying and inducing one person to work at what the others have not learned to handle; on the other hand, as demonstrated above, it is marked by the specialized needs of society, the necessity of exchange, and the pressure of competition.

The first defines division of labor as *terminus a quo*, the second as *terminus ad quem*. As to the qualification of the person, the first rests on the singular, original character of the individual, the second depends in principle upon the equality of individuals, who are called upon to perform specific jobs according to the demands and needs of the surrounding powers. In the division of labor there occurs a characteristic synthesis of the inner vocation by individual qualification with the limitations from external influences, which designate an individual to perform a distinct action even if his talents are quite undistinguished. These two motivations, deriving from different directions, in practice often lack a harmonious bond. What the inner voice desires is often perverted by superpersonal decisions and claims and is arrested in its development. Vice versa, the demands of the objective powers and situations are often completely alien to our gifts, to our actual, specific qualifications.

By the *ordination* of the priest, the priesthood has brought this often abortive attempt at a synthesis to an ideal form, which a priori eliminates all disharmonies. By ordination a spirit, existing in mystical objectivity, is conveyed upon the applicant, making him merely its vessel and representative. Thus his personal qualifications are, on principle, of little concern. The ordination represents admission into a supersubjective communion; it is that definition by an exponent encompassing the personality, which nevertheless defines the subject as if seen from the inside. Here the personality is not commissioned with the task by reason of his special natural preordination (although this might be, of course, one of the reasons and might determine a certain selectivity among the applicants), nor on the chance that he is predestined for this vocation—rather the ordination *creates,* since it delegates the *spirit,* the specific qualification for the task it elects. The saying "To whom God gives an office, he will grant also the knowledge" describes perfectly the condition with regard to the ordination of the priest. The chance luck grants the division of labor in the choice of the specific talents of the subject and its demanding, formative, external powers will be solved by the ordination of the priest—which is, the transference of the spirit a priori. The superpersonal tendency, taking hold of the individual and claiming him for the particular service, in principle prepares his innermost being for these tasks and makes him its absolutely adequate bearer. Here too the religious category represents the ideal type, which reflects the sociological form as in a clear mirror, dissolving its contrariness and reciprocal obfuscation.

The religious social type I mentioned above—the absolute individuality of the individual confronting his God and therefore seemingly unaware of differentiations (as everyone aspires to the same end with the same means, and as no higher unity transforms the individual into differentiated organs)—this type poses indeed a profound problem because of this individualistic form of salvation of the soul. The salvation of the soul should not be understood as a state realized only beyond the grave, but as the gratification of ultimate spiritual longings, the realization of the most inward spiritual perfection, only to be achieved in the soul's struggle with itself and with its god. The soul which has come to its salvation may exist in a terrestrial body or inhabit the beyond—that is an entirely incidental question, as insignificant as that of the location of our domicile, where we meet our fate.

One of the many possible imports of this ideal seems to me of particular significance: the salvation of the soul is only the unfolding, or the exterior realization of, what to a certain degree we already are by nature. What we *ought* to be already permeates as an ideal reality the present, imperfect reality. The soul does not need extraneous help or helpers; all it has to do is to shed its skin, "put off the old Adam," and thus liberate the true kernel of its essence, which has formerly been concealed by sin and imbroglio.

This ideal of the soul as it is intimated in Christianity (although only fragmentarily), and intermixed with quite different tendencies, is characterized by the fact that the projection of our most profound personality—this liberation of the soul of all nonindigenous traits, this self-realization according to the laws of the ego—means obedience to the divine command. The salvation which asked the soul to seek God's favor would not be *its* salvation, but rather a colorless, alienated salvation, if it were not already marked by invisible lines; if the soul could not discover them on its journey to itself.

This interpretation of the salvation of the soul as the redemption, or disenchantment with the values always present in the soul but intermixed with alien, impure, accidental ingredients, seems, indeed, to run into difficulties in the fundamental dogma of Christianity: i.e., the equal potentiality of *every* nature to reap the fruit of absolute salvation, the relativity of salvation through deeds bestowed a priori on everybody. Everyone is welcome in the house of God; for the highest end man can attain is at the same time the minimum that must be asked of him, and it therefore cannot be denied to anyone on principle. Yet if salvation is but the very expression of the soul's innermost being, the pure image of itself, whose ideal form penetrates its earthly imperfection, and if the soul is completely absorbed by it —how is its infinite dissimilarity as to height and depth, width and narrowness, brightness and darkness compatible with the equality of religious blessings, how can everybody be considered equally worthy before God? For our concept of salvation indeed implies the very individual, very dissimilar characteristics of man.

The difficulty of combining equality before God with the immeasurable multiplicity of individuals has led to uniformity of performance, reducing large segments of Christian life to mere schematism. The very individualism of the Christian conception of salvation has been misunderstood, and has also misconceived the fact that everybody shall make the most of *his* natural gifts, because it has insisted on a homogeneous conduct for everybody, instead of letting each be himself. All conformity is contrary to personality; every unity which believers may realize, every equality of the perfected soul, exists only insofar as each single soul animates all worldly accomplishments by *its* particular ideas, and this although the substance of the individual soul may differ infinitely. Jesus suggests in many of his sayings how much he cherishes the diversity of human ingenuity, but he also stresses the fact that this does not necessarily alter the equality of the final outcome of life.

Such a concept of salvation refers to an infinite variety of religious characters, to a religious differentiation, which is not a division of labor; for each individual may attain the totality of salvation by himself, though in a particular way. But the meaning of salvation now turns introspective: the particularity of existence, the feeling of being charged with a unique task and of being put in a place specially predestined for each of us. Thus religious existence is again proven to assimilate and, so to speak, stylize social existence. They are the fundamental categories of our soul, vitalized now by the practical-social aspect and now by the religious aspect. The latter, however, is involved to a lesser degree in the contingencies and cross-relations of heterogeneous interests, and supplements the fragmentary aspects of the practical order by the idea of the absolute. It seems to yield a purer, more uninterrupted presentation of the incomprehensible fundamental categories, so that the religious form of a condition or event is presented as the clarified aspect of a social form, purified of its imbroglio and its clouded, rudimentary essence. Thus art has been defined as the immediate illustration of the ideal prototype of being, while in reality it is but a special form in which these images, like the forms of empirical existence, are realized. But certain forms of representation of these prototypes exhibit an inner purity and perfection, by which they seem to reveal themselves as the true imitation of empirical existence. That, of course, they are not; neither are they the heterogeneous realization of the idea.

It is lack of competition which enables religion to represent the particularity of man, the "next to each other" in variety in *one* realm of perfection. For in the sphere of social existence, competition, it is true, promotes the differentiation of individuals and may help to encourage a wonderful development and close co-operation; yet it is not interested in maintaining this level, for pressing on with the same forces, it carries particularity to an excessive and abortive one-sidedness and to unharmonious grossness. The final goal the religious effort tries to attain and the end every worldly-social toil aims at differ in that the former

61

may not deny its support to any applicant, because it has already granted it to everyone else, whereas in social competition the development of the individual beyond that acme which is determined by his own needs and ideals, does not have to be stressed here. Wherever we find individual differentiations, as defined in this religious sense, they are not as blunt and exaggerated as social differentiations often are, for they are their purer and more perfected counterparts.

V.

The differentiation of the soul, seen from the point of view of the "Kingdom of God," is indeed a form in which the soul will be fused in the unity of this kingdom. In the view of a higher entity it is that form in which, as it were, the elements coalesce into that unity—until finally God becomes the unity of existence as such. He represents this unity of existence, which cannot be expressed by any other definition in regard to both the spatially manifest and the multiplicity of the spiritual. But what is the implication of this concept?

It can be understood as pantheistic, according to which God is identified with the totality of reality. A grain of dust or a human heart, the sun or a flower, all are equally emanations or manifestations of the divine being and enjoy equal rights as its parts. This immanent divine presence already expresses a certain separateness, presumes the autonomy of an external presence which is not God. For every manifestation of existence represents God and therefore every manifestation of his essence is truthfully identical with every other one. Pantheism abolishes the separateness (*Auseinander*) of things in the same way as it does away with being apart (*Fürsichsein*). There is no longer any question of reciprocal action. Its metaphysical, essential unity is immediate and not that of the organism or of society, whose members enjoy unity in exchange for their energies. This god of pantheism is, however, not the god of religion; he lacks that counterpart which man needs to shape his religious mood. Love and estrangement, devotion and being God-forsaken, closeness and remoteness of relation, whose potentiality carries the whole inner life of religion, cease as soon as every point and every moment of existence are thoroughly and absolutely assimilated by the divine unity. Thus this unity must have a different meaning if it is to be the object of a religion. It cannot be directly identified with the material reality of the world.

Apart from this concept of unity, which eliminates all differentiations of existence, rendering all of them identical by identifying them with God, there is only one more: i.e., the above-mentioned unity of reciprocal action. This we call exactly the *one* phenomenon whose elements by virtue of their reciprocally exerted energies cling together, and where the fate of each is dependent upon that of each and every other. This is the unity, the world as a whole, as we conceive it and, setting aside the pantheistic interpretation of the world, it documents itself in symbol and approximation in the organism and the social group. God, imagined as the unity of existence, can be but the representative of this relationship, the reciprocal cause of things, a crystallization into a particular essence caused by them, a crystallization to a point which attracts all the rays of being, the crossroad of all reciprocity of energies and of all relations of things.

Only in this meaning of unity can God, who is this unity, be the object of religion, because only thus does He stand face to face with the individual, confronting him as an outsider and thus transcending him.

The gods we meet as representatives of the energies of the group preform this god of the highest religious level even when they polytheistically embrace individual provinces of interest. Except for Christianity the gods are, if not exclusively at least in part or in one of their aspects, the transcendental images of the unity of the group and should be understood as the unity of the homogenizing, the socializing, *function*. It is true that such a category does not easily yield to analysis; it is the one which the king defined as *"L'état c'est moi."* For this category can never mean pantheistic identity, but it only indicates that the state-forming powers are centered in the king, or that as the representative of this unity he is the counterpart or the sublimation of the dynamic unity of the state. The conceptual process by which God becomes the unity of objects is equivalent to that by which He is known as "love" as such, as "lovingkindness," as "justice" as such, and which supplements the above-attempted derivation of this concept. He *has* these qualities to a lesser degree than He *is* them.

In a pious frame of mind one is inclined to remove the objects by which this pious mood tries to manifest itself out of all empirical relativity and bounds into the absolute, because only thus do they conform to the total width and universal span by which the religious emotion takes hold of the fundamental layers of the soul. Pictured in absolute perfection, each certainty consumes, as it were, its representative; it completely dissolves the being to whom in the beginning it was merely attached. Just as a man who is overcome by a deep suffering, heart-felt beyond all endurance, explains his condition as the impersonation of suffering; just as one says of someone completely beset with passions that he is the personification of passion—so is God seen as omnipotence in absolute dimension, as it were as this quality in substance. Or vice versa: these certainties, imagined in absoluteness and purity, are God; just as they are empirical phenomena when rated relatively and mixed with other positives. Thus the concept of the world as a unity—which can be demonstrated only very incompletely and fragmentarily by the phenomena accessible to us—taken in its absoluteness and, because it does not have to contend with anything unconditional besides itself, becomes a self-sufficient being, we call God: only the limited and conditional needs a representative who, besides being a function, is a somebody, a being. The absolute, the unrestricted, unfettered phenomenon, is free of this yoke.

Depending on the material, which the pious emotion, aspiring to the unity of the absolute, appropriates to itself, the god may be the unity of the universe or the unity of certain manifestations of physical nature or the unity of the group. The group's sociological, reciprocal actions stimulate the forming of that transcendental conception of unity just as much as they create (in the first case) the feeling of the mystical union of all existence and (in the second case) the similarity of phenomena related to each other.

From the point of view of the religious culture of Christianity this genesis of the concept of God, which defines the deity as the absolute of the sociological unity, might seem to be narrow and strange. Here the deity is, on the one hand, the deity of all existence, especially of all spiritual existence; and the separation necessitated by the character of the social group is, in regard to the deity, meaningless and insignificant, indeed altogether antagonistic to this concept of the deity; it is destined to be abrogated by the all-embracing concept of humanity. On the other hand, the God of Christianity is the God of the individual. The road which leads the individual to this God does not expand beforehand into the interstage of the group. The individual stands before his God in absolute self-reliance. The mere sociological interposition is for the concept of the Christian both too narrow and too wide.

For Antiquity and the ethnic world the picture seems quite different. The god of each closed group is its private god, who cares for it or punishes it; and the gods of other groups are accepted as equally real. The individual group does not expect that its god is worshiped like the gods of other groups; indeed, normally it would object most vehemently to any copartnership in the same god as an encroachment on its religious domain with its practical consequences. The group will begrudge other tribes the politically appropriated god, just as it would deny them its own powerful leader or miracle-working sorcerer. This jealousy is an exaggeration of that tolerance which generally characterizes all particular religions. The all-exclusive relation of a par-

ticular god to a specific circle of believers requires the
religious adherents to admit that there are other gods beside
their own—the gods of other groups. Believers in a specific
god are allowed no other gods besides him, not because they
do not exist, rather—to put it somewhat paradoxically—
because they *do* exist (otherwise there would be no reason
for alarm), although they are, to be sure, not the right ones
for this particular group.

We find such a prohibition, amounting to the same inter-
diction, in the political sphere: no one may desert to another
group, and under no circumstances may he abandon his
affiliation with the given social unity. Even the Brahmans
with their pantheistically colored religion heed this tolerance; it is the supplementation of their particularism: They
refuted certain objections of Christian missionaries by
pointing out that their religion might indeed not be congenial to all nations but as far as they themselves were
concerned, it was the right one.

Christianity tremendously revolutionized this solidarity of
the God with the social unity as an always particularistic
trait by rejecting all other gods besides the one it confessed,
not only in its own behalf but indeed in behalf of all the
world. The God of Christianity is the God not only of
those who believe in Him, but the God of the universe. This
God not only lacks the exclusiveness and jealousy of a
personally owned god; the Christian religion indeed is
committed to bringing its God to every soul, for He is anyhow the God of this soul. Conversion to Christianity only
affirms an already established fact. The saying "He who is

not for me, is against me," is one of the greatest turning points of world history in the sociology of religion. Someone believing in Wotan or Vitzliputzli is not necessarily "against" Zeus or Baal: each god is the concern only of his believers; each community is the concern only of its particular god; and the reverence of one group for its god does not, there-fore, infringe upon the sphere of veneration of the others. The God of the Christians was the first to extend His sphere of influence from those who believed in Him to those who did not. Of all the vital powers He was the first to break through the exclusiveness of the social group, which until then had dominated all the interests of its members with its own unity of space and time. The relation to Him in contradistinction to the relation of other human beings or other gods is therefore an exclusive one. Any allegiance to other gods is a positive infringement on the ideal claim He asserts by His absolute monopoly. To believe in other gods means to revolt against Him, for He is also the God of these unbelievers.

Christianity does not concede tolerance. To it tolerance would be as logically contradictory as intolerance is to the particularistic religions. Such a concept of omnipotence, in contradistinction to gods who represent the unity of the social group, is beyond the reach of these groups' imagina-tion. The god of the tribe of Negroes will never do as the god of the Chinese, just as the parents of a Negro can never be the parents of a Chinese child. Neither will a political organization of a closed group be simultaneously the same for another closed society.

69

The unity of the divine being ensuing from this sociological root is probably the precursor of that unity which is attained in Christianity; this development is thus part of those which, having gained their definite state, join in negating and opposing the character of all phenomena leading up to it. The transcending unity of the God of Christianity breaks the sociological limitation, in which the idea of unity has first been raised. The transition of worldly relativities into transcendental absoluteness often transforms the quality of their contents into its opposite. Thus religious emotions depend essentially on that feeling evoked when the believer is confronted by the countenance of his god: love and humility, grace and rejection, prayer and obedience presuppose, as shown already in a different context, an opponent. Although this contrast may be subverted in religious ecstasy, in reality it is but a fluctuation from the unbearableness of complete apartness to the impossibility of complete oneness.

Nevertheless, the concept of God as the absolute substance and energy of being leads to the pantheistic consequence, which annuls completely any being-by-oneself of individual existence. The nearer the soul draws toward the undivided unity with God, the wider, the deeper, the more blissful is its exaltation. But its *complete* absorption by this unity would mean self-obliteration by unrestrained fusion—the soul would vegetate in emptiness. Although all religious feeling clings to its opposite, its very abatement might heighten personal happiness and power; its absolute obliteration, however, would annihilate the entire imaginable meaning and content of religiosity. Thus the sociological-empirical concept of God may lead upward to an always wider aspect of its essence. However, when this process has reached its final goal in the absolute God of Christianity, its content reverts to the opposite of the very sociological character which originally determined the exclusiveness of the god.

The tendency of group unity to assume the form of the transcendental and to equip itself with religious emotional values might be caused by the fact that this synthesis of individuals into a higher form of group unity must only too often seem like a miracle to the more or less lucid consciousness of the individual. In this context personal existence seems to be interwoven in a play of irresistible powers and surrounded by a circle of forces which cannot be explained in terms of its particular elements, and which transcends all of them by a temporal and dynamic circumference, totally lost to view. Law and custom, language and tradition, all that has been called objectified reason, lies before the individual as an immense fund, and his specific share cannot be determined. To all appearances it does not issue from the exertion of individuals but is rather the product of that enigmatic unity which lives a productive life beyond the totality of individuals according to its own superindividual norms. As in nature, here too it is the practical abandonment and the theoretical inexplicableness which cause the religious reaction. And this itself is evidently not characteristic of the group, representing the totality of human beings existing next to each other—for the group itself is not enigmatic; it is tangible and immediate and

71

would anyhow keep reason in the realm of the empirical—but must be ascribed to the fact that this sum is more than a sum, that it develops energies which cannot be found within the individual himself, that from these unities there arises a higher unity.

The membership of the god in the group, the cultivation of religion as a concern of the community, the atonement for individual religious transgressions by the whole group and the group's responsibility for such sins before God—all these typical facts indicate that the deity is the transcendental locus of group forces, reciprocal forces which in reality are at work *among* the elements of the group, and constitute its unity in a functional sense; they have become in the god an independent substantiality. The dynamic of the group life has been carried by the impetus of the religious emotion beyond its individual manifestation and representation into the transcendental, and there confronts these relative individualities as the absolute. The old concept of God as absolute and all humanity as relative here takes on a new meaning. Relations between men here find their substantial and ideal expression in the concept of the deity.

Bringing this analysis to a conclusion, we want to point out that it often lends itself to misunderstandings. This happens if one mistakes the philosophical meaning of things for their origin, their historical development for their objective truth, their logical content for their spiritual significance. The different attitudes of man to his social environment and to his God may therefore manifest themselves in different expressions only with regard to one and the same fundamental category of the human soul, and this is not a temporal condition, in which a spiritual function is transformed by these different manifestations. Each of them is rather a homogeneous fact, which we break up into form and content according to the conceptional faculty of our mind. Its inner structure, independent of its historical contingency, we will have to interpret according to the relation we sense between the inner activity of the soul and the given facts by which it lives. It accretes for us in a timeless process as an expression of its true meaning: from a formal rhythm, from a fundamental movement of our soul and the real or ideal, empirical or metaphysical individual contents of life. And thus all the other not immediately tangible basic tendencies find their more intelligible or veiled, clearer or distorted, expression.

A great number of sociological and religious phenomena, according to their psychical meaning, are often indeed traceable to such common roots in life. Their counterparts, however, originate in the realm of historical-psychological reality. In the language of the temporal and through concrete powers the same truth is expressed, if but fragmentarily, intermingled and broken off by the contingencies of historical reality. These are the innumerable cases, of which I have given a few examples in these pages, where the structure of the social group determines the concepts of the divine essences; where in the relation of men to each other there develop feelings and tendencies which rise psychologically into the absolute, to be written, as it were, in gigantic letters upon the sky.

Thus relations extending into two directions are unfolded: On the one side, the social modes of life manifest themselves as the sources of the religious life and are instrumental in its apprehension. This, in my opinion, is the only useful method of explaining its historical realities. Religion is by its origin certainly not a simple edifice, but—regardless of its unbroken and individual aspect at the height of its evolution—rather a mixture of innumerable motives, none of which by themselves are religion; they grow into religion through expansion beyond their sphere of origin, until they fuse with other motives to form a new model, which cannot be retraced to any one single form. Not without reason each point in the whole circle of psychological impulses has been considered as "the origin" of religion: fear and love, the cult of ancestors and self-idolatry, ethical considerations and the feeling of dependency. Each of these theories is erroneous only insofar as it claims to explain *the* origin; it is correct insofar as it tends to imply *one* of the origins of religion.

To comprehend the origin and the continuance of religion it will be advantageous to unravel from the multiplicity of relations and interests which exist beyond or rather on this side of religion certain religious motives, those rudiments of that which achieved independence and self-reliance as "religion." I do not think religious emotions and impulses are expressed only in religion; they are experienced in manifold combinations upon many occasions, but religion exists as the acme and isolation of the religious element as an independent condition of life. But it will only reach this height when its basic psychological motive has transcended those other forms: e.g., the social, intellectual and aesthetic ones. And on the other side, we notice that developed religious interests present themselves in sociological forms and that these forms become the body for the inwardness of cultic relations, the "next to each other," into which the religious unity will find its way.

However, we will have to exclude most emphatically from these historical motives of the religious aspect questions dealing with the objective truth of its contents. If we succeed in comprehending in the life of man the genesis of religion from the inner conditions of this life, we have nevertheless not yet touched upon the problem whether there is an objective reality, beyond human conception, which comprises the counterpart and substantiation of this psychical reality. This problem is obviously of an entirely different character from the question at hand. But not only the significance of religion in the realm of the objective, but its meaning in the sphere of the subjective, its emotional value, e.g., the effect of the concept of the divine reflecting the innermost feelings, is absolutely independent of all speculations about its origin.

This has caused the crassest misunderstandings of all historical-psychological derivations of ideal values. Many scholars still fancy the charm of an ideal lost, the dignity of a sentiment debased, if its origin is no longer a mysterious miracle, a creation out of nothingness—as if the understanding of "becoming" brought into question the value of the created, as if the lowliness of the point of origin

75

impaired the achieved height of the goal, and as if the unattractive simplicity of individual components destroyed the importance of the product, whose significance is borne out by the co-operative effort in the formation and interweaving of these components. Such is the foolish and confused opinion which assumes that the dignity of man is profaned if it were conceded he is a descendant of an inferior species of animals. But does not his dignity depend on what he in reality *is*, regardless of his humble origin? It is the same sentiment that refuses to acknowledge that religion has its roots in elements which are not yet religion in themselves.

But the very prejudice which tries to establish the dignity of religion by rejecting its historical-psychological source is subject to the reproach of debility of religious consciousness. For man's inner firmness and depth of feeling must be inferior indeed if they are endangered by knowledge of his genesis and will be limited by such knowledge. Genuine and deep love for a fellow being must not be contested by belated recognition of its roots. Such love will show its most triumphant strength by proving that it has survived without scars the death of all these former roots. Equally, the whole strength of subjective religious feeling is demonstrated by the very certainty on which it rests and by which it judges its own depth and sincerity, regardless of its origin.